PET
SOS

Bramble
the
Pony

Tamsin Osler

Photography by Chris Fairclough

W

FRANKLIN WATTS
LONDON•SYDNEY

This edition 2004

First published in Great Britain by
Franklin Watts
96 Leonard Street
London EC2A 4XD

Franklin Watts Australia
45–51 Huntley Street
Alexandria NSW 2015

ISBN: 0 7496 5598 4
Dewey Decimal Classification 636.1
A CIP catalogue record for this book is available from the British Library

Printed in Malaysia

Planning and production by Discovery Books
Editors: Tamsin Osler, Kate Banham
Design: Ian Winton
Art Direction: Jason Anscomb
Photography: Chris Fairclough

Acknowledgements
The publishers would like to thank Liam and Kate Kearns, their children
Hannah, Rhiannon and Conor, their pony Magic, the staff at Glenda Spooner Farm
and the ILPH for their help in the production of this book.

CONTENTS

Meet Bramble

This is Bramble, a ten-year old pony. She lives at Glenda Spooner Farm, a rescue and recovery centre run by the International League for the Protection of Horses (ILPH).

This is Bramble's stall. It has a low door so she can look out.

Bramble is kept in a field near other horses and ponies.

Horses come here for many different reasons. Some, like Bramble, are here because their owners couldn't look after them any more. Some have been rescued from people who were cruel to them. Others are here because they have been abandoned.

The ILPH was set up in 1927. It now runs five rescue and recovery centres in the United Kingdom, and cares for over three hundred horses.

Life at Glenda Spooner Farm

When Bramble arrived at the rescue centre, she couldn't stand properly because she had laminitis, an **inflammation** (or swelling) of the feet. The laminitis was caused by Bramble eating too much rich grass and becoming overweight.

Bramble is checked over by staff.

Ponies and horses spend much of the time eating. This is because a pony's stomach is small, and can't hold a lot at a time. So ponies and horses have to eat little and often.

The vet checks all the animals when they first arrive at the rescue centre. He put Bramble on a diet to help her lose weight.

Bramble has a unique number marked on her back. The police can use this number to find out who owns Bramble and where she lives.

Ponies like Bramble that are born and live in Britain are used to the cold and wet, so they are mainly kept outside. Bramble is put in a field with very little grass so she can't eat too much. These fields are called 'fatty patches' or 'diet **paddocks**'.

There are usually about 60 horses and ponies at the centre. The staff are kept busy feeding and watering all of them.

As well as looking after each animal's needs, the staff also have to **deworm** the horses, **muck out** the stables and keep the main yard clean.

Bramble is being given worming treatment. Horses and ponies need to be dewormed every 6-8 weeks.

All ponies get worms inside their stomach. A few worms will not hurt them, but too many can make them ill. This is why horses and ponies have to be dewormed regularly.

The horses and ponies that are well enough have to be exercised. The staff ride these horses every day.

After riding the horses, the staff clean and polish all the saddles. The **bridles** and **bits** have to be kept clean too. There are saddles and bits for all different sizes of horses and ponies.

The place where all the horse equipment is kept is known as the 'tack' room.

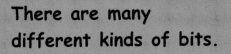

There are many different kinds of bits.

A new pony for Hannah

This is the Kearns family. They already have two horses, which Mrs Kearns rides. Now they want to get a rescue pony from Glenda Spooner Farm for Hannah, her eldest daughter, to ride.

Mrs Kearns with her three children, Rhiannon, Hannah and Conor.

Hannah wants to learn as much as she can about looking after a pony. She and her sister like to look at pony books.

There are many things to think about before getting a pony. Keeping a pony is a lot of hard work, and can be very expensive. If no one in your family has kept a pony before, your local stables or riding school may be able to give you advice.

The Information Centre at Glenda Spooner Farm.

Hannah and her family visit Glenda Spooner Farm. First, they look at the books and equipment on display in the Information Centre.

Hannah is shown a book about the different parts of a horse's body.

Then they go to the stable blocks and the paddocks. One of the staff introduces them to Bramble, who is the right size for Hannah to ride.

Before the Kearns can take Bramble away, an ILPH field officer will visit their home to make sure that Bramble will be safe and happy there. If the field officer approves their home, they will be able to fetch Bramble as soon as they like.

The vet's visit

Before Bramble goes to her new home, she is checked over by the vet. He makes certain that her heart and lungs are working normally.

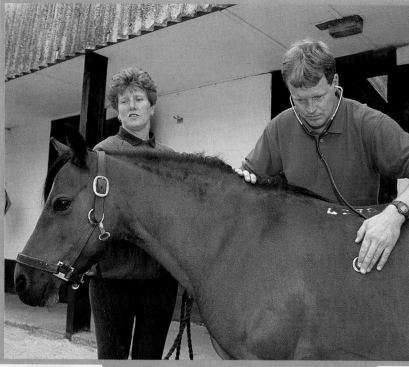

The vet uses a stethoscope to check Bramble's heart.

He checks her teeth, and uses a **rasp** to file the sharp edges off them.

The vet also looks at Bramble's feet to make sure they are healthy. Finally, he gives Bramble any **vaccinations** she needs.

The vet checks Bramble's feet for any signs of soreness.

Bringing Bramble home

Bramble arrives at her new home in the family's horse box.

Hannah has brought her new pony home. She leads Bramble down the ramp of the horse box and into the stable yard.

Horses are **herd** animals, so they like to be near other horses and ponies. Hannah's mother takes Bramble into the field where she keeps the other horses.

Ponies like to be with other ponies, but donkeys and sheep are company too. If you don't have a suitable field for your pony, you may have to keep it at a **livery** stables.

Hannah's mother carefully leads Bramble to meet another horse and its foal.

Caring for Bramble

In spring and summer, Hannah has to make sure that Bramble doesn't eat too much rich grass. If she became fat again, she might get another attack of laminitis.

Hannah fits a fly net on Bramble.

Flies are a nuisance in summer. Hannah puts a fly net on Bramble to protect her from them.

In winter there isn't enough grass in the field for Bramble to eat. The girls fill a hay net with hay. Then they hang it up in Bramble's stall.

Ponies like to be fed and watered at the same time each day. The amount and type of food a pony needs depends on the **breed** of the pony and how much exercise it gets.

Sometimes Hannah also feeds Bramble with **horse nuts**.

A pony's coat changes with the seasons. In winter it grows long and thick. In spring the pony 'moults' (loses its winter coat), to leave a new short and smooth coat.

One of the jobs Hannah enjoys most is **grooming**. She uses a special brush to remove any dirt and mud from Bramble's coat. She also brushes Bramble's tail. Grooming helps Hannah and Bramble get to know each other well.

Before she goes riding, Hannah removes any dirt from Bramble's feet. She uses a hoof pick to do this. It doesn't hurt the pony.

Next, Hannah's mother helps her put the saddle and bridle on Bramble. It is important that everything is put on correctly. The saddle must be fastened securely and the **stirrups** must be set to the right length.

Hannah's mother watches carefully as Hannah and Rhiannon fit the saddle on Bramble.

Learning to ride

Hannah learns to ride in a special
area filled with a deep layer of sand.
This is called a **manège**.
Hannah can now ride
around the manège on
her own. She has won
lots of rosettes at
pony events.

Hannah always wears a helmet
when she rides Bramble.

When her sister, Rhiannon, rides Bramble, her mother holds a very long rein called a **lunge**. She uses this to guide the pony.

Horses and ponies need regular exercise to keep healthy. A pony that doesn't get enough exercise may become too lively and difficult to handle.

Conor gets his turn on Bramble as well.

Hannah can now trot on her own.

At least twice a year, an ILPH field officer will come to check that Bramble is healthy and being well looked after. Hannah's family never know when a field officer is going to visit, but they always know when he has been because he leaves them a card.

Hannah spends a lot of her free time looking after her pony. This helps her to understand how Bramble thinks and why she behaves in certain ways. It will help Hannah to become a better rider too.

Bramble is very happy in her new home. The family give her lots of care and love, and Hannah and Bramble have become the best of friends.

Glossary

Bit	The piece of metal that fits inside a horse's mouth. It is connected to the reins and helps the rider to control and steer the horse.
Breed	A type of horse. British breeds include 'Shetland' and 'New Forest' ponies.
Bridle	The leather straps that a horse wears on its head.
Deworm	To remove worms from a horse's stomach.
Grooming	Brushing a horse to remove dried mud and sweat. This helps to keep a horse's coat in good condition.
Herd	A large group of animals that live together.
Horse nuts	A specially-prepared food for horses.
Inflammation	A part of the body is said to be inflamed when it is swollen and sore.
Livery stables	A stables where you pay to have your horse or pony housed and looked after.
Lunge	A long rein used to make the horse or pony walk round the riding instructor in a circle.
Manège	An enclosed and safe area at a riding school where people are taught to ride.
Muck out	To clean out the stables.
Paddock	A small field where ponies and horses are kept.
Pony	A small horse, less than 14.2 hands high. Horses are measured in hands. One hand is equal to 10.16 cm.
Rasp	A file with a rough or jagged edge.
Stethoscope	The medical tool used to check the heart and lungs.
Stirrups	The loops that support a rider's feet.
Vaccinations	Medical treatments that protect people and animals against particular diseases.